STUFF EVERY
GRANDFATHER
SHOULD KNOW

Stuff Every
Grandfather
Should Know

by James Knipp

QUIRK BOOKS
PHILADELPHIA

Library of Congress Cataloging in Publication Number: 2018943042

ISBN: 978-1-68369-100-6

Printed in China

Typeset in Adobe Garamond and Brandon Grotesque

Designed by Elissa Flanigan
Cover illustration by Molly Egan
Production management by John J. McGurk

Quirk Books
215 Church Street
Philadelphia, PA 19106
quirkbooks.com

10 9 8 7 6 5 4 3 2 1

Stuff Every Lawyer Should Know: The publisher and author hereby disclaim any liability from any injury that may result from the use, proper or improper, of the information contained in this book. We do not guarantee that the information is safe, complete, or wholly accurate, nor should it be a substitute for the reader's good judgment and common sense. In other words: Exercise caution when fielding unsolicited grandparenting advice. Be über-prepared for tantrums, piggyback-induced muscle strain, and unsuccessful implementation of "when I was your age" anecdotes. And never underestimate the power of a well-timed cookie.

To Lily Jane, without whom this book wouldn't be possible

ADVICE, WISDOM, AND RELATIONSHIPS

FUN, PLAYTIME, AND SPECIAL TREATS

Introduction

grand•fa•ther

> *n:* 1. the father of one's mother or father.
> 2. a forefather; an ancestor.

We all have an idea of a grandfather: an elderly chap sitting in an easy chair dispensing pearls of wisdom, usually starting with "back in my day . . . ," from behind an open newspaper. But a grandfather is more than a cartoonish image, more than the father of your parent.

When I learned that I was going to be a grandfather I thought I had another few years before I took on that particular role, and the life I had hoped for my daughter didn't include having a child at such a young age. But when the day arrived and this beautiful little life-form came squalling into the world, she stole my heart and I swore I would do everything I could to be the best PopPop possible.

In some ways, it's been easy. Watching my baby granddaughter transform into a beautiful little girl has been a joyous adventure, and I'm looking forward to sharing the next few decades as she grows into a wonderful young lady.

In other ways, it's been harder than I thought. Managing a household full of adults, teenagers, and children is a challenge no matter how much you love them. But I have found—thanks to the perspective and patience I've gained by this stage of life—that I'm a better PopPop than I was a father. And through experience, meeting other grandfathers, and researching this book, I found that a grandfather can be many things.

He can be a fortysomething man who wears graphic tees and plays Dungeons & Dragons on the weekend. He can be a construction worker a decade away from retirement, with calloused hands and a warm heart. He can be a second father who fills a void when required and stands back when that vacancy is filled. He can be a grandfather through marriage or adoption who loves his "instant grandchildren" as much as he loves kids who share his genes.

He can be a shoulder to lean on, a jester or judge, a secret-keeper or truth-teller. A grandfather can be whatever his children and his children's children need, whenever they need it. I have been many of these things and more as a grandfather, and I've gained my own pearls of wisdom on the way. As you embark on your own adventure with your grandchildren, I hope they work for you as well.

What Kind of Grandfather Are You?

All kinds of people can become grandfathers at various stages in life, so it's no surprise that there are many different styles of grandfathering. And like most mysterious endeavors in life (parenting, interpretive dance, vlogging about snack foods), you don't know exactly how you'll tackle it until you're deep into the practice—until now! The following quiz uses dozens of minutes of research to help determine your "grandpa-sona."

Which of these Father's Day gifts would you like most?

   a. A box set of Harry Potter movies
   b. A tie and cuff links
   c. A subscription to a genealogy website
   d. A shiny new toolbox
   e. A shot glass that reads "PopPop Fuel"

It's your eight-year-old grandchild's birthday. What do you pick up as a present?

   a. Tickets to Disney on Ice
   b. A sturdy new pair of shoes
   c. A day at a museum
   d. The kid's first tape measure
   e. A book called *1001 Experiments to Gross Out Your Parents*

What are you listening to right now?

    a. Rock and/or roll

    b. Something classic and orchestral, like a nice Bach cantata

    c. NPR or light jazz

    d. Nothing. It's hard to hear over this table saw!

    e. A humor podcast—and it skews a little blue, if I'm being honest

What's your favorite '80s movie?

    a. *The Princess Bride*

    b. *Wall Street*

    c. *Stand by Me*

    d. *Platoon*

    e. *Weekend at Bernie's*

What's your favorite weekend chore?

    a. Rearranging my CD collection

    b. Balancing the checkbook

    c. Organizing my bookshelves

    d. Putting a dent in the ol' "honey do" list

    e. Chores? That's what I had kids for!

If you answered mostly As . . . you're the Cool Grandfather: This is the easygoing, hip-and-with-it grandfather who gets his grandkids. Need someone to chaperone the class trip, go fishing, or attend an invitation-only princess tea party? He's your guy. Willing to drop all at the child's beck and call, this cool cat will enhance the next generation's musical taste and introduce the youngster to the best in graphic tees, old-school television, and movies from the '70s, '80s, and '90s.

If you answered mostly Bs . . . you're the Chief Executive Grandfather: This guy believes in boundaries. And order. And turning off lights when you leave the room and loading the dishwasher the right way and pretty much anything that keeps the forces of chaos from overrunning the world. The CEG understands that everything has a place and that those who run a tight ship sail for happier shores. He may seem stern, but this grandfather provides vital lessons about discipline and routine.

If you answered mostly Cs . . . you're the Teacher Grandfather: Speaking of lessons, this grandfather finds them everywhere. Part family historian, part storyteller, this guy is a walking, talking Wikipedia. You'll frequently find him with his nose buried in a book or a newspaper (or even a tablet). He's your go-to guy whether you're writing a book report, in need of relationship advice, or dying to know why cousin Myrtle always wears that weird hat.

If you answered mostly Ds . . . you're the Handyman Grandfather: You'll often find this guy puttering around his basement workshop, garden shed, or kitchen table covered in clutter. He can fix anything from a busted radio to an unwound cassette tape (hey, you might listen to it again one day!). Often the most patient of the grandfatherly types, he has a tool for everything, a belief that the best lessons are learned over a workbench, and a never-ending supply of duct tape.

If you answered mostly Es . . . you're the Funnyman Grandfather: Teller of jokes, both dadly and off-color, this guy puts the *fun* in funny (and sometimes dysfunction). Never one to take life too seriously, this grandfather will don silly hats, engage in rip-roaring tickle fights, and doggedly ask you to pull his finger. Always there to remind you that age is a state of mind and it's never too late to have a second childhood, the Funnyman Grandfather is the guy you want to visit when you're having a crappy day and need the ol' frown turned upside down.

Of course, the best grandfathers know that different situations require different types and find a way to combine all of these elements, so figure out which style suits you best . . . and then improvise.

Grandfather
Basics

How to Pick Your Grandfather Nickname

You're going to be a grandfather! Congratulations. You've got no shortage of important decisions to make about visits, vacations, finances, and so on. But no choice is as significant as what you will be called.

Your grandfather nickname is the bedrock of your grandfather identity. How you determine your nickname can vary across generations, regions, and quirks in your grandchild's pronunciation that may leave you with a nickname you regret. Regardless, here are a few ideas to get you started.

The Classics

Grandpa: The old standby. Occasionally accompanied by a second name (such as Grandpa Beaky) to distinguish between two or more Grandpas. Favored among the older grandfather set.

Gramps: This nickname is simple and effective, with just a hint of irony.

Papa: A cozy storybook name with a retro vibe, perfect to accompany Nana or Mama. (Also: Pa, Poppa, and other derivations.)

Pops: With a bit of '50s flair, this works especially well if you're the neighborhood guy who owns the corner store.

The Old Man: A little hardcore for most tastes, this one is usually assigned to you by a less-than-admiring relative. Wear it with pride (or irony).

Regional Relics

Grumpa: Mostly seen south of the Mason-Dixon Line. Said by some to be perfect for an "ornery, old conservative" with a heart of gold.

PawPaw: A spicy Cajun classic, with added *w*s for extra-long vowel sounds.

PopPop: A favorite in the northeast U.S., with various spellings, spacings, and capitalizations (e.g., Pop Pop, Poppop, Pop-Pop, and so on).

Poppy: Made for the old-money, New England set (to wit: this is what George W. Bush calls George Senior). Better have a trust fund ready if you go with this one.

Cultural Monikers

Papik: Armenian

Pépère or **Grand-papa:** French

Pappous: Greek

Opa: German

Saba: Hebrew

Nonno: Italian

Ojiisan (formal) or **Sofu** (informal): Japanese

YeYe (paternal grandfather) or **Wai Gong** (maternal grandfather): Mandarin Chinese

Dziadek: Polish

Abuelo: Spanish

Daadaa (paternal grandfather) or **Daadi** (maternal grandfather): Urdu

Zaide: Yiddish

Dedushka: Russian

Babu: Swahili

Just Plain Silly

PSquared: For engineers or mathematicians

G-Dawg: For the grandfather who likes bling, has an old rap hit, or is a big *Walking Dead* fan

Grand Dude: For surfers, West Coast royalty, and fans of *The Big Lebowski*

Pooples: Slightly mocking suggestion from an old friend (just wait until he has grandkids)

Dad's Dad: Ideal for grandkids who want to be as precise as possible in describing their relationships

HipPop: One for the millennial grandkids. Perfect for the grandfather who loves artisan bread, microbrews, and trendy beards.

Grandmeister Pop-N-Duffer: For the grandfather whose holds irony most dear. Use this one if the "other" grandfather steals your first choice.

Baby-Talkin' Grandpas

Sometimes you don't have a say in the matter and the kid christens you. Any Gampy, Gamps, Gampa, Gwampa, Da Pa, Bappa, Bappy, Baboo, or Dranpa will tell you: you just gotta roll with it.

How to Help on Delivery Day

The fateful day has arrived and your grandchild is about to enter the world. Childbirth is no easy task, but as the grandfather you can serve a few roles in order to keep things running as smoothly as possible.

Backup/emergency driver. Make sure your child and their partner have your contact info (including work/daytime numbers if appropriate), and do some preliminary route-planning to their place and then to hospital (some mobile GPS programs let you save a route, allowing you to call it up quickly when you need it). If you end up as chauffeur, drive safely, obey traffic laws, and don't panic. Although a swift delivery is possible, it's relatively rare, and you'll put everyone at risk if you take corners on two wheels. And don't feel like you have to play the hero; if you're truly worried about the baby arriving on the way or about any other serious complications, pull over and call an ambulance.

Security detail. Babies are hospital celebrities. An unending line of aunts, uncles, coworkers, and friends—not to mention the other grandparents—may be clamoring for that first glimpse of the newborn (especially if this is a first child), all while Mom is exhausted and just wants private cuddle time with the baby. With the parents' blessing, you can man the velvet rope and coordinate who gets in and out. Don't be a jerk about it; a simple, honest "they're resting right now" will do. And don't let the power go to your head, or you might find yourself on the other side of that velvet rope.

Communications chief. Someone has to get the word out, and who better than the guy who has everyone on his contact list? You can make those phone calls and share phone snapshots with your other children, friends, parents, and the folks in your child's inner circle. (As always, make sure the parents are OK with all your shares, especially anything you put on social media.)

Babysitter. If this isn't your first grandchild, watching over her older siblings can be a truly clinch role for Grandpop. You may not be first to see the new arrival, but you might be present for the first time the siblings meet each other—and the parents will no doubt be grateful for your help.

Instant Grandchildren: Blended Families and Beyond

Everyone knows the so-called traditional path into grandfatherhood: your kids have kids. But that's not the only way to take up the grandfather mantle. You could marry into a family that already has grandchildren, or your child could adopt or marry someone with kids. These family-building journeys can be complicated, maybe even awkward, but there are many ways for you to maintain cohesive and loving relationships with everyone involved. Read on to become the best newly minted grandfather you can be.

Offer time and patience. Having a new grandparent can be difficult, especially for an older child. He may be confused about this new relationship, or he may think establishing a relationship with you is disloyal to his biological grandparents. He may be impatient or even hostile toward you. Don't take it personally. Be patient, be yourself, and give him time. Chances are, after he comes to know you as a supportive and loving presence, your new grandchild will see you for what you are: another part of the family.

Treat everyone equally. Humans are a tribal species, and it's easy to divide newly formed groups into "us versus them" camps. But it's important that you treat step-grandchildren or adopted grandchildren with the same love and affection as you would biological ones. This means everything from spending quality time together to giving gifts; when shopping for holidays or birthdays, make sure gifts are similar in value, personal appeal, and thoughtfulness. (Also see the Grandfatherly Art of Gift Giving on page 110.) Playing favorites is a surefire step toward driving a wedge into your new family.

Get rid of the "step-." Regardless of how they came into your life, these are your grandchildren, period, so always introduce and refer to them as such. Get your own grandfatherly nickname, one that works for both you and your new family, and let the kids know that they can absolutely treat you like a biological granddad. Likewise, if your new grandchild is adopted, she's not your "adopted granddaughter," she's your granddaughter. Refer to her "biological parents" or "birth parents," never her "real" parents.

Manage expectations (yours and those of others). It might take time for new family dynamics to feel comfortable, so although you may be overjoyed at the arrival of grandchildren, the kids won't necessarily feel the same right away—or ever. Let the kids know you

are here and consider them your grandchildren, but
don't immediately order matching family sweatshirts
or start planning holiday photos. You may end up
being more of a friendly background figure to the kids,
and that's okay; don't push a relationship. If possible,
become acquainted with their biological grandparents
so the kids know you're all on the same team—theirs.

Keep it to yourself. You may want to complain to your
child or stepchild about your new grandchildren. Or
you may feel an urge to compare their activity and
accomplishments to those of your biological descen-
dants. Don't. If there is trouble, chances are the parents
know about it, and the worst thing to do would be to
pile on and harp—it's passive-aggressive and a direct
route to hurt feelings. This isn't to say you can't have a
conversation about the relationship you hope to have;
just keep it constructive and don't criticize. Think "I
want to be part of their lives" instead of "your kids
are so rude!"

Five Things No One Will Tell You About Becoming a Grandfather

When it comes to grandfathering, it might seem like there's nothing to it but to do it . . . right? Here are five time-tested truths about your new patriarchal role that aren't *quite* so obvious.

It sure ain't the same as fathering. With much of the day-to-day dad duties taken care of, your role is more advisor and ambassador than parent, negotiating the dangerous straits of family dynamics.

Adult children can be a pain in the tush. Of course you love 'em, but once your kids beget kids of their own, they suddenly become stubborn and are always sure they know what they're doing . . . even when they're clearly clueless. You were never like that, were you?

You find new appreciation for your father and grandfather. Because you *were*, in fact, like that, and now you start to understand exactly why your old man (and his) did and said the things he did. (Sorry, Dad.)

Age is irrelevant. The thought "But I'm too young to be a grandfather" gives way to basic math when you realize that (1) you're about the age your father was when your kids were born, and (2) the only reason you remember your grandfather as being "old" is because when you're little, everyone over the age of 30 is ancient. And that's when you realize, to your grandchild, you're ancient too (and that's OK)!

I'm not jealous, you're jealous. When you're a dad, there's little competition for the wee one's affections—most of the time, it's just you and maybe Parent #2. But as a grandfather you're often relegated to a supporting role, and you may be one of four (or more!) grands competing for a cheek pinch. That's just the nature of things—and something to make peace with.

Kid Care and Feeding 101

You've raised kids already, but depending on where you are in life, it may have been years, even decades, since you've had little ones about. Here's a refresher on the must-knows.

How to Change a Diaper

- Carry the baby around and try to hand her off to someone else. No, just kidding—a good grandpa knows when it's time to step up.

- Have your supplies (clean diaper, wipes, cream) ready and within arm's reach.

- Lay the baby faceup on a secure, flat surface and make sure she stays there—a gentle hand on the tummy will keep her from wriggling too much. Never leave her lying alone, especially if she's on a table. Give her a fun, distracting toy to hold while you do your thing.

- Unfasten the diaper and remove it. Depending on the size of the mess, you may be able to use the cleaner section toward the front/top of the diaper to corral the material in the center. Wrap the used diaper into a tight little ball and seal shut for later disposal.

- Use wipes to clean the diaper area, remembering to wipe from front to back to avoid spreading bacteria.

- Apply a little diaper ointment if you see chafing or redness.

- Wait for her skin to dry, then put on the clean diaper. You can do the classic "scoop up by the ankles" to place the new diaper under her tush or lay the front on top first to prevent surprise showers (especially from boys). Fasten securely.

- Parade around like you've just completed one of the marvels of modern engineering. Grandfathers rule!

How to Set a Baby Down for a Nap

- If your grandchild already has a routine, learn it from the parents and try your best to stick to it.

- A baby's sleeping space should be free of pillows, stuffed animals, and crib bumpers, which can increase the risk of suffocation. Likewise, the sleeping surface should be firm enough for him not to sink.

- A baby sleeps on his back every time. Tummy sleeping puts him at risk for sudden infant death syndrome.

- Do not overdress the little sleeper. A single swaddle blanket is enough (or less, if it's hot).

How to Feed Your Grandkids

- For babies who are bottle-fed, the simplest way to make sure you're giving them what they're used to eating is to ask your child to prepare the bottles ahead of time. Keep these refrigerated and never heat them in the microwave. Otherwise, buy the same formula that your grandbaby gets at home to avoid tummy troubles.

- For babies who are breast-fed, Mom will provide you with breast milk in small bags. If it's frozen, thaw it overnight (at least 12 hours) at room temperature or in a bowl of warm water. Again, no microwaving—it can destroy nutrients in the milk.

- Begin by sterilizing the bottle with a good wash in hot, soapy water and allow it to dry completely. Once filled with milk or formula, seal it and warm it, either by running it under hot water or by setting it in a bowl of hot water. Then gently shake the bottle to mix hot and cool spots. That old-fashioned squirt test on the underside of your wrist still applies: if it feels hot to your skin, it's probably too hot for the baby.

- For older grandbabies who've graduated to pureed baby food and cereal, again, it will be simplest to have your child pack whatever she wants the baby to eat. But also keep a list from your child on hand of what foods you can serve. Be cautious about introducing new foods—check with Mom and Dad first. Remember: infants under the age of one should not eat honey because it can carry botulism that their young immune systems can't fight off.

- Kids under age 5 have a higher risk of choking, so if you're on food duty, make sure their meal is bite sized. Hot dogs, apples, grapes, and raw carrots should be chopped into small pieces or, better, slivers. Most nuts, popcorn and hard candy are no-nos. Don't give these to your grandbaby until she's older.

Food No-Nos

Know all your grandchild's food allergies by heart, and check ingredients closely; allergens like nuts, soy, wheat, and milk are found in a wide variety of foods, and even small amounts can cause a reaction. Prevent cross-contamination in your kitchen and cooking area by washing up thoroughly after consuming an allergen, and don't be shy about speaking up in restaurants. If your grandchild's food allergy is severe enough to warrant it, make sure you have the appropriate medicine (Benadryl and EpiPens are the most common) on hand in case of a reaction, know how to use it, and know how to call a doctor or emergency line for help.

Foods may be off-limits for religious or moral reasons too. Honor the wishes of your grandchild's parents (even if you don't agree with them). It's not your place to introduce those foods to your grandchild.

How to Soothe Teething Pain

- Give the infant something cold to numb her gums, such as a cold (or even partially frozen) wash cloth. Don't give her an ice cube, which is a choking hazard.

- Pop in a teething ring if you have one. (Some types can be frozen, too.)

- Sometimes just your (clean) finger might be enough. Gently apply pressure to the sore parts of her gums.

- If your grandchild is over 2 years old, topical anesthetic like Orajel or Anbesol can work wonders. This is not recommended for younger infants because of an increased risk of a rare, serious condition called methemoglobinemia.

Kid Safety 101

Once infants start to toddle, the fun really begins. Remember when you were a new parent and you spent weeks trying to childproof your living space? The following reminders will ensure you keep your grandchild secure while he's in your care.

Safety in the House

There's little in this world more curious, or deceptively quick, than an active toddler. If you have a grandchild between the ages of 1 and 5 coming over, make sure your house has been childproofed.

- Covers for electrical outlets are required and can be found in your local hardware store or online.

- Medicine, cleaning supplies, and sharp objects should be moved out of the reach of little grasping hands. If you don't have another place to store them, install cabinet and door locks. (A zip tie will work in a pinch—just cut it off after he leaves.)

- Safety gates allow you to block off entire rooms (for example, to keep a boisterous pet out of kiddo range). You can choose from several types, but simple pressure-style gates are the easiest to install and store.

- If you have furniture with sharp corners, install safety bumpers to protect little noggins. Any beloved, breakable accent pieces should be moved to a higher shelf, because grandkids are basically heat-seeking missiles for your most expensive knick-knacks. Consider locking up electronics like your cable box or security keypads because toddlers cannot resist the blinking lights (and no one wants to reprogram the DVR again).

- Before your grandchild arrives, do a sweep through the house for small objects that could present a choking hazard.

- Furniture and appliances must braced to a wall. Televisions, bookshelves, and dressers are especially dangerous to climbing children, so pick up braces at a hardware store or online and make sure they're installed properly.

- Obviously, if you own firearms, they should be unloaded and locked away at all times regardless of how old your grandkid is.

- If you have a workshop, make sure power tools are unplugged and out of reach.

Safety in the Car

The National Highway Traffic Safety Administration (NHTSA) recommends that children through age 12—yes, 12!—should be in a car seat or booster until they fit a seat belt properly, so if you're going to be driving your grandchild a lot, you may want a dedicated car seat for your vehicle. Check any model for recalls or updates before purchasing, and avoid buying second-hand if you don't know the seat's complete history; even if the model is up-to-date, if it has been in an accident it could have sustained hidden structural damage. Car seats can be expensive, but making sure you have a new and certified model is worth the expense.

The type of car seat you need varies with age, and there are convertible models that can adapt as the child grows. The NHTSA recommends the following:

- Kids ages birth to 12 months require a rear-facing carry-on-style car seat. These can usually be placed into and removed from a locking base that you can leave in the car, and some models even have a matching a stroller attachment. These are good for children who weigh up to 20 pounds.

- Keep your grandchild rear-facing for as long as he is within the height and weight limit for the seat.

Sometime between 1 and 3 years, he will begin to be too big to fit comfortably in a rear-facing model, at which point he can graduate to a forward-facing car seat. Most use the vehicle's seatbelt system to hold the car seat in place and an independent belting system holds the child in the car seat.

- Between the ages of 4 and 7, your grandchild will be ready for a larger, or full-seat, booster seat. These raise her a little higher in the seat and guiding the car's seatbelt straps to more safely restrain him.

- From ages 8 to 12, kids become ready for smaller, simpler booster seats that help them sit higher in their seats. These can be used in conjunction with special harnesses that slide onto the seatbelt straps to ensure they don't slide off shoulders or across necks.

- All cars built after 2002 are required to include (relatively) easy-to-access bars to attach all standard car seat designs. Although installation may still require acrobatic agility beyond the range of mortal humans, overall these seats are much easier than those earlier versions that led to a generation of early-onset backaches!

- Children should remain in the back seat until they are over five feet tall. Though airbag technology has improved, the force of the supplemental restraint system (SRS) can hurt smaller passengers. And of course, under all circumstances, your grandchild must wear a seatbelt—as should you.

Little Kid Milestones

Chances are it's been a few years since you raised a child, so your memory of developmental benchmarks and when they occur might be hazy. Here's a quick refresher.

Age	Physical skills
2 months	Can lift head and chest when lying down
6 months	Can roll over and sit up, first tooth comes in, can begin eating solids
12 months	Crawls or scoots well, stands independently, takes first steps
18 months	Runs well, molars come in
2 years	Can throw overhand and kick a ball, most teeth are in
3 years	Can pedal a tricycle, can climb stairs
4 years	Can hop
5 years	Can skip, can dress self

Social skills	Grandpop response
Smiles back at you	Clear extra space on your phone for photos
Able to baby talk	"Whooo's da prettiest baby girl . . ."
Knows singular words	"Say PopPop . . . c'mon . . . say PopPop!"
Scribbles with crayons, enters "terrible twos"	Buy extra fridge magnets Freeze some towels to help with teething
Speaks in 2-word combinations, knows about 50 words	"This one has a cannon for an arm. Hello, sports scholarships!"
Speaks in 3-word combinations, you understand about 75% of what she says	"Why do you want to eat a bug? Oh . . . tub . . . you want to get in the tub. Got it."
Can draw "potato people," can handle some organized sports/classes	"Oh, that's me? With an eye patch? Love it."
Can write name and hold conversations	Pack extra tissues for the first day of school

How to Go from Father to Grandfather

Think grandfatherhood is merely an extension of fatherhood? Think again. You're older now and hopefully a little wiser. So whether you've gained new knowledge about what's important in life or you're just too tired to give a damn, chances are your attitude has changed about a number of things.

Use this handy chart to easily convert fatherly positions to grandfatherly ones.

Father says	Grandfather says
You broke *what*?! You have to learn to be more careful.	Eh, this old thing? I was going to throw it out anyway.
You can't watch cartoons; I'm watching the game.	Sure, you can change the channel. It's only the playoffs.
Please pick up your toys.	Leave that. I'll put it away later.
Please stop this racket! I can't hear myself think!	I think this drum set is a perfect gift!
Eat what we serve—we're not running a restaurant here.	Mac and cheese again? Whatever my princess wants.
You're not getting a toy every time we go to the store. Don't even ask.	Of course I can buy that for you. How about the whole set?
No dessert until you clean your plate.	Life is short; eat dessert first.
Go ask your mother.	Don't tell your mother.

How to Create the Perfect Bedtime Routine

Maybe your grandchild is hopped up on the sugar you poured into her. Maybe your home is unfamiliar, full of frightening shadows and missing the key comfort items she has at home. Whatever the reason, you are exhausted and your spawn's spawn has suddenly decided she is a night owl and refuses to sleep. These are the essentials to help you usher your beloved grandbaby into dreamland.

Her favorite stuffed animal/blanket/toy. The comfort provided by a favorite item can often work wonders for an anxious sleeper, so remind your child to pack it. You can also keep a backup lovey at your house—just have a story ready to explain slight variations in her favorite teddy's appearance.

A photo of Mom or Dad. It seems simple, but sometimes your grandkid needs a reminder that Mom and Dad will be back soon—especially if nights away from home are rare. A photograph placed by her bedside can ease her worries.

A script. Structure and routine are important to children, so try to mimic your grandchild's normal bedtime routine as much as possible. Keep her bedtime the same as when she is at home, and if she does things in a certain order at home (drink milk, then brush teeth, then read a story), adhere to that order.

Storytime. A good bedtime story (or two or three) is often the perfect way to end the day. Pick something with minimal excitement, and avoid books that require "audience participation" (this are good during the day, but not when trying to wind down). Read slowly in a soft voice, and always remember to say "The End." (For more storytime tips and recommended bedtime reads, turn to page 103.)

Monster repellent. Kids have active imaginations, and new places and experiences can set them in motion. Oddly shaped furniture, toys and blankets, even photos on a wall can spark scary thoughts, so be ready to rearrange and create a monster-free zone. Pick up some "monster spray," aka a plant spritzer, air freshener, or even a spray bottle filled with water. Announce to your grandchild that you are bringing this to the battle against the monsters, and spray liberally under beds, behind dressers, and into closets.

Sleepy songs. Sometimes a little soft singing is all it takes. It doesn't matter if you can't carry a tune, it's all about tone and pitch. Keep your voice soft. Classic lullabies often work, or you can make up your own tune. You might not win a Grammy, but you might just find yourself up for a "Grampy"!

Snuggles. Sometimes your grandchild needs extra TLC, and grandfatherly cuddles are among the most effective tools in your shed. Don't be surprised if you fall asleep too.

How to Work with the "Other" Grandparents

One of the most surprising relationships you'll develop as a grandfather is the one with your grandchild's other grandparents. Depending on family dynamics, personalities, and distance, they may be your new best friends . . . or irredeemable boors who represent everything you hate about people your age. Whatever the case, they're still your partners in grandparenthood, and you'll need to learn to work in tandem with them. Here's how to make the most of the relationship.

It's not a competition. I get it, we're guys, and everything is a competition. But this is one footrace that ends only in frustration (and possibly gift-buying-induced bankruptcy). You may find yourself comparing yourself to the other grandparents especially if there's a difference in finances, location, or availability, but ultimately you can only affect *your* relationship with your grandchild. Maybe you can't buy him the same things or spend the same amount of time as your counterpart, but you bring your own skills to the table. So celebrate those differences.

Try to be friends. Chances are you have more in common with your fellow grandfather than you think, such as similar life experiences and feelings and uncertainties about being a grandparent. At a minimum, you have your grandchild in common, so start there. And if for some reason friendship isn't an option, try for mutual respect, and always . . .

Behave and take the high road. Maybe you're a liberal snowflake still touting a Hillary 2016 bumper sticker and he's a MAGA-hat-waving loudmouth. You don't have to be friends (not everyone is), but remember that no matter what, your grandchild's needs come first. Birthday parties, family picnics, and holidays are not the place for arguments, political or otherwise. Don't bring up hot-button issues, and don't take the bait if your counterpart does. Avoid harping to your child or child-in-law about the other grandfather. Chances are they know the score, and complaining will only put them in a bad spot.

Working with Your Coconspirator

If you are a very lucky grandfather, you'll have the benefit of a partner in crime. Your significant other is a key contributor and ally whom you should never take for granted—especially at this new life stage. And just as parenthood gave you new challenges along with new joys, grandparenthood will present its own set of unique tensions, dramas, and interpersonal problems. That's to be expected—and doesn't mean your relationship is on the rocks!—but to make the going get a little easier, here are a few ways to forge a grand partnership in your new roles.

Remember you're a team. As new parents, you probably did almost everything together. Now that you are older, you and your spouse may have settled into separate roles, but that doesn't mean one of you will be in charge of all grandparenting. Make sure you're helping out with day-to-day stuff, especially babysitting, and do your part to keep on top of dates, planning, and logistics for special events like birthdays and school performances.

Be flexible. Whether your partner needs you to play the heavy in a tough situation or lighten the mood when levity is needed, be ready to adapt and support as necessary. Your whole family is reconfiguring around a brand-new life-form; now's not the time to be a stick-in-the-mud, especially because the two of you are likely to become go-to resources for any new-parent crises.

Talk the talk. Don't bury your face behind the newspaper or tablet. Speak to your spouse, as openly and honestly as you did when you were courting (do people still court?). Talk about your concerns and fears and dreams about your new life as a grandpop—chances are, if it's making you feel old, or overwhelmed, or anxious, your spouse might be feeling the same way. Don't shy away from the tough topics like money, retirement, inheritances, medical decisions, and end-of-life plans, and don't forget to tell her she's still beautiful—grandmother or no.

Listen. Don't fall into the "yes, dear" trap. Pay attention when your spouse is speaking, don't disregard her concerns, and don't try to solve those concerns (unless asked). She may have a legitimate need to troubleshoot something like planning a grandchild's birthday party or a holiday dinner, or she just may need a friendly ear for her grandmotherly frustrations.

Stand up when necessary. If your child, their partner, or even your grandchild is walking all over your spouse, be an advocate for her. If she is tired of last-minute babysitting duty and misses going to her book club, offer to take over once in a while, or privately tell your child that Nana needs some time off.

Laugh out loud. Humor is important, and grandparenting is full of its fair share of hilarious mishaps. In short, don't take yourself so seriously.

Advice,
Wisdom, and
Relationships

How to Give Parenting Advice

Dr. Spock—and the internet—can't answer everything. So whom can parents turn to when they need advice or are at their wit's end with their brood? Who has the experience, the wisdom, the problem-solving genius to swoop in to the rescue? Well, probably Batman, but because he's not available, there's always you, the wise grandfather. Giving advice is an art—you don't want to step on toes, hurt feelings, or boss anybody around. Follow these guidelines.

Remember what worked . . . You probably made a lot of good choices as a dad. How did you deal with tantrums and bedtimes? What things did you do that ended with a smile or helped your child learn something new? These techniques form the basis of good advice.

. . . and what didn't. Perhaps you wish you'd had more patience, or you now see that an issue that seemed vital at the time was ultimately not a hill worth dying on. We all make mistakes, and it's tempting to sweep them under the rug and act like you got it right from the get-go. Resist that temptation; instead, share your parenting failures as well as your successes, plus what you would have done differently if you knew what you know now.

Change with the times. Fifty years ago, corporal punishment was considered acceptable, even necessary, for disciplining children. Now, years of study have proven otherwise. The parenting trends of your generation may be just as out of style . . . and maybe never worked in the first place, so think twice before you recommend infant Mozart CDs or communal sleeping sacks. You don't need to know the details of every parenting fad out there; just have a basic understanding of what methods have been determined to be most effective and nurturing.

Make it judgment free. Parenting is hard enough, and no one likes being second-guessed. Be kind when you're sharing your knowledge. Saying "This worked for me" instead of "you're doing it wrong!" will go a long way toward helping your child without making him feel defensive. Never crack jokes to the effect of "now you know what it's like" or "see what I had to deal with?" Your kids were *kids* when you raised them, and parenting isn't some kind of retribution for all their youthful tantrums.

Don't take it personally. So you've offered your heartfelt, no-judgment child-rearing advice—and your child promptly rejected it. It's easy to take that as a repudiation of your beliefs and experiences. Don't.

Sometimes parents want (or need) to figure things out on their own. Maybe they'll eventually come around to your way of thinking, or maybe they'll learn something that they can teach you.

Timing Is Everything

Advice giving is just like comedy; it's all about timing. Here's when to share your wisdom.

The worst times to give advice

- When they are in the middle of an argument with their child or spouse

- When they are in the middle of correcting/disciplining their child

- When they are angry, frustrated, and in need of space

- When they have already heard and rejected the same advice many times

The best time to give advice

- When they ask

Five Golden Nuggets of Parenting Wisdom to Share

So, what child-rearing advice would I offer my children? I'm glad you asked. Here's what PopPop KnippKnopp has found to be universally true.

Have patience. Every regret I have about raising my children involves losing my cool and berating them for some relatively minor offense. Remember, mistakes happen, and yelling at someone won't fix them.

Forget the small stuff. If your child wants to sleep upside down in bed or wear cowboy boots to a fancy party, let her. As long as she's not endangering herself, let her be silly. It will make everyone happy, and in twenty years, it won't matter that she wore fairy wings to class picture day.

Make time. This can be hard when you're young and the kids are young and the world is moving 1,000 miles an hour. But I've found that the first twenty years of your child's life can pass in a heartbeat, so be sure you carve out the time to make moments and memories.

Listen and observe. Sometimes the things your child tells you may seem unimportant or trivial, but it's vital that you *really* listen. What your kids are saying (and sometimes what they're not) is important to them, so it should be important to you.

Laughter truly is the best medicine. Life is way too short to be taken seriously. Don't be afraid to make fun of yourself, and try to find something to laugh about every day. There's a reason that dad jokes exist: though they bring eye rolls and heavy sighs now, they also bring smiles and memories.

What to Do When You're Overruled

One of these days you're going to want to give your grandchild a piece of candy, or take him out to the rickety pier to fish for barracuda, or do some other brilliant thing that your child simply does *not* want you to do. This can be frustrating. After all, your kids turned out all right, right? Plus, grandfathers are meant to spoil their grandchildren. It's like one of those unwritten rules in baseball people get riled up about.

Here's how to balance wanting to make your grandchild happy with avoiding the wrath of his parents.

Know the no. Your child may have a perfectly good reason for saying no. Maybe they have diet or health concerns about their kiddo eating that treat. Maybe your precious angel was acting less than precious or angelic before you arrived, and his parent doesn't want to reward his behavior right now. Talk to your child and find out why they disagree with your suggestion; at the very least, it'll help you plan appropriately in the future.

State your case. If your child offers no particular reason for rejecting your plan, don't harangue or nag or make accusations. Simply explain your point of view; there may be room for negotiation. Remind your child how much quality time meant to her at that age or mention a recent achievement that you think earned your grandkid an additional award. Try to work out a compromise—save the candy for tomorrow or relocate the fishing trip to a safer spot.

Accept it. If your child continues to say no, move on. Don't sneak behind your child's back, and *never* team up with your grandchild by making his parents the enemy.

How to Live Together without Losing Your Mind

There's no place like home! So much so that your children and their new family may return to your humble abode. Or perhaps they never left, preferring the familiar and free to the scary and expensive. Or maybe you're moving in with them. Living in a multi-generational household with your kids and grandkids (and maybe their significant others) can be a rich and rewarding experience . . . or a chaotic, hair-pulling nightmare filled with bitter recrimination, tread-upon feelings, and years of therapy. Here are a few pitfalls to watch out for and ways to make them right.

Problem: no space. Furniture, photos, toys, and clothes can clutter up even in the most organized household. Even something as simple as groceries can become a challenge when everyone insists on having their favorite items and fridge space is tight. And lack of breathing room can make alone time rare or impossible.

How to fix it: Establish rules on bringing new stuff into the house (for example: for every new thing brought in, one old thing must be given away). Set up a menu and grocery schedule for adult household members, and take turns purchasing and cooking for the week.

If possible, give everyone their own space to retreat to, and respect closed doors—just because you're their parent doesn't mean your adult child wants you barging in on them. Likewise, if there are times of day when you're not up for kid-watching or chitchat, make that clear to the rest of the household.

Problem: routines are no longer routine. Prior to sharing space, you might have watched the news every day after work, but now your television has been taken over by a cartoon sponge and his starfish friend. Or you like to shower and shave at 7 a.m., but your son-in-law commandeered the bathroom at 6:55 and isn't leaving any time soon. Whatever the specifics, you'll likely find that your routines will be disrupted when you start sharing space.

How to fix it: Discuss schedules and timelines that are important to the family; for example, timing is less negotiable for people heading off to work or school, so give those folks priority when needed. These rules don't have to be military-rigid and could be as simple as setting TV limits or taking your shower ten minutes earlier. You may have to be flexible and create new routines (after all, the news is depressing, and that sponge guy is hilarious).

Problem: it's getting messy (in many ways). With limited space and disrupted routines, things can literally pile up quickly. Chores become a challenge, dishes go unwashed, resentments grow, and you find yourself either biting your tongue or mediating UN levels of intrafamily conflict.

How to fix it: Make a chore list and set expectations for who will do what each day—in writing if necessary. If cast-off clutter is a problem, set out a box in a common area and throw stuff in there when you come upon it, with the expectation that the owner will tend to it before the end of the night (and if not, the box will end up square in the middle of their bed—their stuff, their problem!).

Problem: you're having second thoughts. Any big life change can prompt a "grass is greener" mind-set, but in the case of living together, it's often a necessary change that can't be easily undone or changed. Still, all the friction can add up and make you (and everyone else) bummed out and stressed.

How to fix it: Remember that living multigenerationally has many advantages. You have ready access to your beloved grandchildren. Your kids now have built-in babysitters they can trust. You rarely need to worry about leaving an empty house when you take a trip. Having extra adults in the house means you have game night partners, grocery getters, maybe even drinking buddies. Perhaps most important, you have a daily opportunity to create memories, pass down stories, share laughter, and gain allies against life's many challenges.

How to Be a Great Local Grandfather

If you live close to your grandchildren, consider yourself blessed. Although technology has made it easier to stay in contact in a variety of different ways, nothing beats physical proximity to help maintain a close relationship with your grandkids. Here's how to make the most of being a local grandfather.

Set a good example. The best way to be a great local grandfather is to live right! If your grandchildren see you treat them and their parents with respect and good humor, genuinely enjoy their company, and generally be a good person, they're going to want to spend time with you—and, perhaps most important, follow your lead.

Drop on by. Why wait for an invitation? Stop by for a coffee. Help out with chores. Or just hang out and chat. The earlier you establish a presence in your grandchildren's regular routine, the more integral you become in their lives. Of course, make sure random stops are OK with your child, and be sure not to abuse this privilege or overstay your welcome.

Offer to babysit. Parenting is hard, and every parent needs a break now and then. Volunteer to keep an eye on your grandkids for a few hours so your child can run errands, work out, or spend some time alone. Or make it an overnight stay so the parents can have a date night. Not only does babysitting give the parents much-needed adult time, it helps you and your grandkids stay close. If you stop by every Saturday so that Mom can grocery shop without packing up the kids, you will be a familiar and comfortable part of the family.

Stay involved. Find out what activities your grandkids participate in and attend their dance recitals, little league games, and other events. They'll feel supported and loved when they spot your face in the crowd, and your presence will go a long way toward helping them get the most out of their activities and learn new ones. For more tips on being their best booster, turn to page 106.

Offer to chauffer. As the kids get older and more involved in school, sports, and their social lives, shuttling them around becomes a chore unto itself . . . especially in families that have more than one kid. If you have a vehicle and time in your schedule, offer to relieve the parents of driving duties. You could have a routine—say driving them to school every morning—or be available in case of an emergency.

Drive time has the extra bonus of being talk time

too. Ask about what's going on in school, meet their friends, and hear about their likes and dislikes. And when they are learning to drive, offer to help them practice. Your grandkids may be less nervous with you in the passenger seat than with a parent, and you'll earn some points to cash in later when you can no longer drive!

Schedule Grandpop time. Develop a regular "thing" with your grandkid, such as a monthly matinee, a standing Saturday lunch date, or a puzzle that you work on together when she comes to your house. Anything works as long as it's an excuse for just the two of you to get together. Use that time to listen to her: to let her tell you about her normal day, what she's experiencing, what she's learning, and so on. Unless she asks, go easy on the "when I was your age" stories. Grandpop time should be about her.

Your grandkid may opt to keep this time going even through the angst-filled years into adulthood, but don't be surprised (and don't take it personally) if her interest wanes. This happens. Treasure the time you have shared, and who knows—when she gets older and more settled, she might want to continue your regular sessions.

How to Be a Great Long-Distance Grandfather

You may find yourself anywhere from a few hours to a whole country away from your grandchild. Distance can be difficult, but we live in an age when technology can bridge most divides and help you stay involved in your grandkid's life. Here's how to keep connected no matter how far apart you are.

Social media is your friend. Social media has its drawbacks—privacy concerns, fake news, the occasional uncomfortable overshare—but it's unmatched when it comes to connecting people across distances. If your grandchild is a ways away, stay on top of her (or her parents') Facebook, Twitter, or Instagram feed. Don't smother them, but do chime in from time to time with congrats or compliments when appropriate (and whatever you do, don't become a compulsive meme sharer—no one likes those guys).

Schedule a regular chat. A weekly phone conversation or video chat doesn't have to be exhaustive, but rather a routine opportunity to check in, talk about your week, and maintain a relationship with your far-flung descendant.

Texting isn't just for teens. Kids live on their phones, and there is probably no better way of connecting with your grandchild than via text messages. No need to be intrusive, but a casual "what's up? I'm thinking of you" might be enough to set up a quick conversation. Teens can be fickle, though, so expect occasional delays, and don't take it personally if you don't get a response. Also, be conscious of school hours; you don't want to get your little darling in trouble with her teacher.

Game together. If you and your grandchild enjoy video games, you can bond virtually. Many games allow users from all over the world to connect and play together. Suggest a dedicated time, perhaps outside of her usual forays with friends, when you can save the world (or conquer one) together. If you're not a console guy, consider a simple mobile-device game, like Words with Friends.

Kick it old-school. In this digital-first world snail mail has become the exception, but it's still the gold standard for truly personal communication. Every now and then, send your grandkid a longer note written on paper. Keep it light and maybe tell a story or send a few photos. Paper birthday cards can also be a fun treat to look forward to. Speaking of which . . .

Don't forget special events. Keep a birthday reminder tacked to your refrigerator and send her card a week ahead of time. Ask your child to let you know when other big occasions (sports, school plays, recitals, etc.) are approaching, and check in with a quick "break a leg" (unless she's playing football). If you're in gift-giving mode, you can have wrapped gifts sent directly to your grandchild at the click of a button, even if you can't deliver them in person.

How to Set (Fair!) Rules

The conventional wisdom is that grandfathers have only one rule for their grandchildren: that there are no rules. But in practice this leads to utter chaos, and you can set boundaries while still maintaining your position as the coolest adult in your grandchild's life. Follow these guidelines.

1. **Establish a baseline.** Discuss with the parents their rules for the child regarding television and computer use (both content and how much screen time is allowed), limitations on video games, bedtimes, and other behaviors and privileges.

2. **Determine what your rules are.** Now that you have a baseline, you need to determine exactly what your boundaries are and why. Are you trying to keep your grandchild safe? Protect some semblance of peace and quiet of your home? Knowing your reasoning can help later when discussing rules with your grandchild. Make sure your rules are age appropriate.

3. **Set expectations early.** This doesn't have to be formal, but have a conversation with your grandkid up front to walk through what's off-limits

when you are together. And be prepared to explain why, especially with older kids. Providing a vague answer will do nothing but kick-start their curiosity and all but guarantee that a particular line will be crossed.

4. **Communicate the consequences.** Make sure your grandchild knows what will happen if she breaks a rule. The ramifications can be anything from "I'll tell your parents" to "I'll bake you into a pie," but maybe the most effective is simply conveying the deep disappointment you'll feel if she doesn't comply (never underestimate the power of guilt).

5. **Offer alternatives.** When you explain what's off-limits, also point out the things your grandkid can do. For example, if television is unavailable after 7:30 pm, maybe she can play a game instead.

6. **Be ready to lay down the law.** What happens if your grandchild crosses one of your boundaries? Well, there's always the pie option, but that only works once. There are a number of less cannibalistic ways to address your little rule-breaker.

- **Talk it out.** Depending on the offense, you might only have to explain why the rule exists and how your grandchild's actions make you feel. Be prepared to listen to her feelings as well.

- **Give her a time out.** The old standby still works, especially with younger kids. It's less about punishment and more an opportunity for the little wrongdoer to consider what she did and why it was wrong.

- **Confiscate a prized possession.** Sometimes there's no better way to create repercussions than to temporarily take away something she cares deeply about like a toy or an electronic device. Be prepared for pushback here.

- **Call in backup.** Calling in the parents should be a last resort—after all, you're watching the little rug rat to give your child a break. But if the offense is egregious or rule-breaking is habitual, you may need to bring in the big guns.

How to Handle Separation and Divorce

Considering that conventional wisdom (not to mention the American Psychological Association) tells us that nearly 50 percent of all marriages end in divorce, there's a good chance your family will face this scenario. The fallout from divorce impacts families, including grandparents and grandchildren, in many different ways and can be bitter. Here are ways you can strive to preserve a relationship with your grandkid once the dust settles.

Keep out of it. This doesn't mean you can't have opinions or support one side or the other (or perhaps both), but for the sake of your grandchild try to stay neutral. Make sure your home is a safe place free from recrimination and blame that your grandkid can retreat to even after the split is finalized. And *never* use the opportunity of a visit to bad-mouth your child's ex.

Be supportive. Obviously, divorce can be stressful, and your grandchild (and your child) may need more support from you than usual. Offer to babysit or run errands while the parents work out the proceedings. Be a shoulder for your grandchild to lean on. Discuss his fears and concerns. Reassure him that his parents still love him and that you'll continue to be in his life. Although it may be difficult, work with your child and your former in-law to make sure the kid's needs—emotional, mental, and physical—are met.

Stay positive. Divorce can be traumatic, and your grandchild may need to hear that things will be all right. Be truthful—lying about the divorce and saying his parents still love each other are perhaps the worst things you could do—but remind him that he is loved. Tell him that many parents remain friendly after a divorce and that, no matter what, he has your support. Your grandchild may act out during this time, so prepare to be patient and absorb the shocks.

Be willing to share. Holidays can be especially tough for grandchildren whose parents divorce. There are many people to visit and many chances for hurt feelings. Stay flexible with schedules and traditions. Work with your child to alternate holiday visits, or plan a separate celebration the week before or after the holiday. Thanksgiving on a Friday night can be just as special, and your willingness to compromise will make things less stressful for everyone.

If you're the one getting the divorce

Although breakups among us older types are rare—a 2017 Pew Research study based on US Census Bureau data found that only 10 in of 1,000 married people over age 50 (or 1 percent) divorced in 2015—the number of so-called gray divorces doubled between 1990 and 2015. Here's how best to support your grandchild in the event that you and your spouse divorce.

Watch the finances. A 2016 Bowling Green State University study found that gray divorces led to greater financial insecurity. Manage your affairs carefully, particularly as they relate to your grandchild's future.

Be mature. You and your spouse may have gone separate ways, but always be courteous in person. Withholding support, be it financial or emotional, because of a grudge towards your ex-spouse can be destabilizing to the whole family and is like cutting off your nose to spite your face—or, in this case, your grandkid.

Respect the relationship. If you find a new significant other, expect resistance from your loved ones and give them time to adjust. Time may heal all wounds, but in the meantime, be respectful of others' feelings and make sure everyone is on board before you show up to a family event with someone new.

Silver Linings for Gray Divorces

If you've ended your marriage, it's not all Sturm und Drang. Look for these positive spins when life throws you this particular curveball.

You've learned life lessons. Nothing teaches like experience, and ending your marriage could give you a new perspective that ultimately strengthens future relationships, including those with your kids and grandkids.

Sometimes you need a reboot. If your marriage was unhappy, it probably negatively impacted your whole family. Now you've now hit reset and gotten a fresh start, which could set everyone on a path to greater happiness.

You can stand stronger. In your marriage you may have adopted particular roles and ignored others, and some life skills may have atrophied. Now is an opportunity to become a well-rounded individual by relearning old skills, reawakening forgotten parts of yourself, or acquiring new knowledge and experiences.

Grandfathers as Guardians

According to a 2016 PBS NewsHour report based on US Census Bureau data, 2.7 million grandparents nationwide are primary caregivers to their grandchildren. You've already been a parent, of course, but raising your grandkids involves new challenges and considerations. Here's how to be a good guardian.

Follow the rules. If you are raising your grandchild under court order, it's important you follow the requirements set forth by the judge, including those regarding parental visitation. Doing so may be difficult or emotional, especially if it's your child whose access to the child is restricted, but breaking these rules could endanger your grandchild or result in him being put under another family's care.

Be honest (but not judgmental). If your grandchild asks why you are responsible for him, be honest without judgment and don't bad-mouth his parents. Explain that not everyone is ready to be a parent, people make mistakes, sometimes tragedy happens—whatever is appropriate to your circumstances.

Talking to Kids about Drugs and Alcohol

If the issue is drugs or alcohol, have an honest, age-appropriate discussion with your grandkid.

- Preschoolers typically don't need details. A simple "Mommy or Daddy needed some help, so they asked me to keep an eye on you" will do. Always provide reassurances that he is safe here with you.

- For a grade-school kid, frame the parent's behavior in a blame-free way, reminding your grandchild that this is not his fault and that his parent is not a bad person but someone with a disease who is getting help.

- Teens may be the toughest to talk to. You can discuss the struggles his parent experienced (or continues to experience), but do so without condescending; teens are smart, and if they don't learn about drugs and alcohol from you, they'll learn elsewhere. Support groups such as Alateen can help teens cope by finding community with their peers.

Look to the future. Let your grandchild know that just because his parent struggled doesn't mean he has to follow the same path. Remind him that his parent's absence has no bearing on his worth and that you love and support him.

Get help. Raising kids is exhausting. Raising a grandchild can be doubly so, depending on your age and his. Many states offer financial help and healthcare options for adults raising their grandchildren. Your local library, AARP.org, religious communities, senior centers, schools, and other organizations may provide resources ranging from free or low-cost counseling to financial services to babysitting and playgroups. And if you have friends and family willing to pitch in, take advantage. You shouldn't have to do this alone.

How to Stay Healthy, Wealthy, and Wise

If you are not already over the hill, there is a good chance that you are at least approaching the summit. Grandfathering tends to be a second-half-of-life thing, and with that come the cares and concerns of becoming older, including changes in your finances and in your physical and mental health. Sometimes these can be challenging, but these steps can help you live your best grandfather life.

Staying Healthy

Whether because of a "man up" attitude or a general dislike of doctors, some of us don't think about our health until the loss of life or limb is literally imminent. But as men of a certain age, we have to be on the lookout for the big three—diabetes, heart disease, and high blood pressure—and a plethora of other aging-related illnesses and ailments. And yeah, no one lives forever, but these tips will help you ensure that whatever quantity of years you have left is filled with quality.

See your doctor at least once a year. Don't wait until you're sick, and be honest about your lifestyle, symptoms, and any concerns. You may have spent a lifetime being told to tough it out, but now is the time to consider your doctor the pit chief whose main job is to keep your engine roaring for as long as possible in this NASCAR race called life.

Take chronic conditions seriously. Follow your doctor's advice on diet and lifestyle. Make taking maintenance medication part of your daily routine, somewhere between shower and shave, and don't skip doses. Know the potential side effects and report them to your doctor as appropriate.

Document your medicines and dosage. Keep track of everything you are prescribed, and share that list with all your doctors, pharmacists, and significant other. Your phone's notes or health app is an excellent place to store this information, since it's portable and easy to share.

Watch for the "big three." Diabetes, high blood pressure, and heart disease are the most common health problems men face later in life—but they can also be prevented or managed healthfully.

- **Diabetes:** Tell your doctor posthaste of symptoms like urinating often, feeling very hungry or thirsty, blurry vision, cuts or bruises that are slow to heal, and tingling, pain, or numbness in the hands or feet.

- **High blood pressure (or hypertension):** This condition is often symptomless; get your blood pressure checked regularly to screen for it.

- **Cardiovascular disease:** Early symptoms can be few and far between, but regular cholesterol checks can raise a red flag. If you start experiencing shortness of breath, numbness or weakness in the arms or legs, or severe tightness or pain in the neck, chest, or jaw, seek immediate medical attention—many men aren't diagnosed with cardiovascular disease until they have a heart attack.

Eat right. Remember when you could down six chili dogs chased with a pitcher of beer in one sitting? Those days have passed. Learn to love leafy greens, save desserts for special treats, and switch to whole-wheat bread. Changing your diet doesn't have to be painful; for example, if you're a champion grillmaster, try swapping your steak or sugary BBQ ribs for veggie kabobs and lean chicken.

Stay active. It's far too easy to fall into the sedentary cycle of bed, desk, couch, repeat. But the National

Institute on Aging recommends that seniors (and soon-to-be seniors) get at least 30 minutes of activity that ups your breathing rate every day—i.e., you're working hard enough to make conversation a bit challenging but not impossible. Try small tricks for increasing your activity like parking farther away from building entrances, getting off public transit a few blocks early, walking or hiking on weekends, and taking the stairs rather than an elevator. Of course, you can still go the gym route via either a standard health club or a discounted (or free!) program for seniors from a local community center. Check with your doctor before embarking on any new exercise or nutrition program.

Staying Wealthy(ish)

Perhaps you've reached a stage in life where you have financial stability, your mortgage is paid, and you're able to help your kids and grandkids financially. Not everyone is in this boat, and many grandfathers live paycheck to paycheck. No matter your situation, it's never too late to establish good fiscal habits.

Write up a formal budget. Seems simple, right? But it's often easier said than done. Step one is to know where your money is going: for one month, track all income and expenses. Use an app like Mint or You Need a

Budget, a spreadsheet, or go old-school and write it out with pencil and paper. Mark the things that you can't do without (mortgage, insurance, groceries, car expenses) and be honest with yourself about everything else (dining out, unused memberships, subscriptions). Use this info to create spending expectations—and then stick to them.

Downsize. If you live in a big house with a big mortgage, taxes, and maintenance costs, consider moving to a smaller, cheaper house or apartment, especially if you're an empty nester. If you have a vehicle (or two) that you rarely drive, consider selling it.

Save. Although experts recommend that adults over age 50 have five times their annual salary saved, 70 percent of American adults have less than $1,000 in savings. So if you feel behind, you're not alone. And it's never too late to start. Conventional wisdom says to save 10 percent of your income, but that can vary according to your earnings, budget, and age, so if you're unsure, start small and have, say, 5 percent of your income transferred to a bank account that you cannot readily access, such as a savings account that limits monthly transactions. Then just forget it's there. If you receive a regular pay increase, increase your savings by that amount before you get used to seeing it in your check. Participate in your company's retirement plan (especially if they have an employer match—that's free money!). If your company doesn't offer a retirement plan, look into putting money into an IRA for similar savings benefits. (IRAs also offer a "catch-up" rule that allows savers over age 50 to invest an additional $1,000 per year over the $5,500 limit.)

Ask for help, part 1. Numerous federal and state programs are aimed at helping people who have fallen behind financially, especially seniors. Visit your local library, senior or community center, or state government website for information on programs available to you for anything from discounted heating services or transit fare to cheaper prescriptions. If you're older than age 55, check AARP.org for resources. You may feel a social stigma associated with using these measures, or you may just feel old, but such programs and laws are in place specifically for helping people in your situation. And you've probably paid for many of these services for years via taxes.

Ask for help, part 2. Seek support from your adult children in small ways (such as adding you to their family cell phone plan) or large (such as offering to share living space). This may be hard, but don't let pride get in the way of your financial security.

Staying Wise

Grandfatherhood often happens in a time of transition. On one hand, things seem to be constantly changing. You're getting older, you've spent your life being "The Man," and your kids are adults bringing new life into a world that seems to be moving faster and faster every time you look up. On the other hand, you feel like you're standing still. Your daily routine, especially if you are retired, can become so, well, routine that it stagnates and you find yourself in a rut. So what's a grandfather to do with this mixed-up, bifurcated perception of the world? I'm glad you asked.

Ask for help, part 3. The US Centers for Disease Control and Prevention estimates that 20 percent of people age 55 or over experience some sort of mental health concern, including depression and anxiety. As men, we've often been trained to bottle up our emotions, so when an issue like this affects us, we may be inclined to refuse to address it. But asking for support can be a game-changer. If you're feeling overwhelmed, know that you're not alone. Senior centers often offer support sessions and groups that can help you connect with others in a similar life stage who share your concerns. Also seek out a licensed therapist (you can often find one through your healthcare provider's web portal). In some cases your sadness may be transient, and in others you may find medication helpful for getting through it.

Rediscover your significant other. If your empty nest is affecting your emotional well-being, your partner may be feeling the same. You may have spent half a lifetime focused on your kids, but now it's time to relearn everything about your better half. Take a trip, sign up for a dance class, or just make a point to hang out in your pajamas together once a week. (Also see Working with Your Coconspirator on page 49.)

Rediscover your secret talent. Maybe you're a writer, artist, or musician but you've always put that pursuit on the back burner to focus on raising kids and earning money. Now is the time to bring it to boil, as either a second career or just a hobby. History is filled with talented folks who found their calling later in life, and there's no reason that can't be you!

Volunteer. Maybe your talent is helping others. Perhaps you're a financial wizard who can help less-advantaged folks balance their checkbooks or a gung-ho server ready to feed the homeless at a local soup kitchen. There are tons of meaningful opportunities for you to help make the world a better place.

Network. Join a common-interest community. There are literally hundreds of them, from book groups to cooking seminars to groups dedicated to beagle puppies. Search online on sites like Meetup.com, or check your local library or senior center.

Never stop learning. Sharks need to keep moving forward to survive. Brains are the same way: learning new skills keeps your mind from atrophying. So take time to learn something new. Check out local community colleges, night schools, and even retailers—for example, many home improvement stores offer one-day seminars on deck-building or gardening. Or, to really mix things up, learn new technology. Imagine the surprise and wonder when your grandchild finds that you already know all about whatever new app is blowing up the interwebs!

How to Prepare for Your Future (and Theirs)

The future is coming. And as you know from raising your kids, it gets here awfully fast. The following advice can help prepare you and your grandchild for a stable future.

Put money aside. If you're in a position to do so, try saving money that your grandchild can use when she reaches adulthood. It doesn't take much: a mere $25 per week capitalized over 18 years at 5 percent interest would result in $35,000! There are various vehicles and investments, including:

- **529 plans:** These allow you to put money aside tax free for education expenses. Several types exist, including options that let you purchase pre-paid credits from a participating university. The more traditional education saving plans work almost like a retirement account, in which you select various investment vehicles (like stocks, bonds, or mutual funds). The biggest risk with these plans is that any funds used for non-college-related expenses are taxed at an additional 10 percent penalty.

- **Roth IRAs:** These individual retirement accounts allow your investments to accrue tax free. Unlike traditional IRAs, contributions to a Roth IRA are not tax deductible, but you have greater flexibility to withdraw funds for things like for college expenses without penalty. If your grandchild doesn't go to college, the funds can remain untouched and serve as a retirement account down the road.

- **UGMA/UTMA accounts:** Uniform Gift or Transfer to Minors Act (UGMA/UTMA) accounts are a way to hold money or securities in trust until your grandchild turns 18 (or 21 in some states). These tend to be less flexible, and the taxation implications, which vary by state, are often greater.

Invest in long-term care (LTC) insurance. As you age, your costs for medical care can rise precipitously. Medicare and health insurance can help with a portion of your expenses, but nursing home costs, assisted living, or hospice and respite care may not be covered by your plan and, even when they are, the copayments and deductibles of elder care are often prohibitive. An LTC insurance policy can offset some of those costs.

Research your options; premiums can be pricey, but having something in place now can prevent you from struggling later.

Have your papers in order. A will can help prevent complications with your estate later (even if you don't feel like you have an "estate"!). Most lawyers can whip up a standard will quickly and cheaply, but do-it-yourself options exist if you don't want to incur a fee; find recommendations for both writing a will without an attorney and local law office referrals at ACLU. org (search for "estate planning resources"). Consider making an end-of-life plan for your medical care (like a do-not-resuscitate order) or arranging a prepaid funeral, so your survivors don't have to worry about tough decisions or large expenses.

Get rid of it early. Consider doling out family heirlooms, important keepsakes, or just practical stuff you no longer use, like household appliances in good working condition. In the best case, handing down a storied piece could become a treasured memory for your children and grandchildren, and in the worst, you save them the agonizing decision of what to do with your stuff once you're gone. Try to document what you are giving and tell the story behind it so the receiver knows its meaning. Have picture parties where you go through old photos and catalogue the contents (who, where, and what), so your ancestors can treasure the memories and in turn pass them down. Don't weigh family members down with stuff they don't want; Aunt Mildred's prized collection of stuffed waterfowl may spur fond memories in you, but to your children and grandchildren they're just some moth-eaten birds that will take up space in an attic. Be prepared to let some stuff go. Let family have first dibs, then donate or sell the rest without regret.

Get your online life off-line. We put a whole lot of our life on the internet these days, and your posts and pictures may end up outliving you by decades. Perhaps you want this (it is, after all, a form of immortality), but online scammers could use your accounts for nefarious purposes. Tap one of your survivors to take care of your online life. Provide a list of your most recent log-ins and passwords for social media, internet services, and other aspect of your online life. Some social networks even let you appoint a "guardian" to look after your account after you pass away.

With all of these options (except maybe your Facebook photos), it's wise to talk to a financial planner, who can advise you on tax implications, logistics, and the best overall approach for you and your family.

Fun,
Playtime,
and Special
Treats

How to Tell a Tall Tale

As one of the older players in your family circus, at some point you will be called upon to share a story. About how you met your wife, about your grandchild's parents, or maybe about the "good old days," which may seem as distant and far-flung to the younger generations as ancient Rome is to you.

When that time comes, you have a choice. You can tell it like it was, as dry and clinical as a study in astrophysics, or you can spin a yarn that will entrance your grandchildren and may be passed along for generations. Before you start worrying about being truthful, remember that any tale told from memory is going to have some degree of falsehood; it's the way memory works. So why not have fun with it?

Start with a kernel of truth. Sure, it's fun to spin a yarn about wrasslin' a grizzly or eating fifty flapjacks in a sitting, but the best tall tales have a real story at their cores. Your baseline doesn't have to be an important part of the story, but it should be something that happened. Even if you don't consider yourself the wild type, you probably have at least a few anecdotes from your past that are ripe for embellishment. For example:

> "One time I met a very pretty girl at band camp. Her name was Amanda, and we hit it off surprisingly well (especially considering how awkward I was around girls as a teenager) . . ."

Add a splash of action. You'll want a little conflict to move the plot along—after all, nothing is more boring than a story of endless "and then . . . and then . . . and then . . . " When the story starts to drag, insert a reversal of fortune or an unexpected obstacle, and feel free to exaggerate a little. Real life is often mundane, so if stretching the truth leads to a better tale, stretch away. Do so sparingly, though; too much drama will make you sound like an action star and diminish your audience's ability to suspend belief.

> "We only knew each other for a week, but what a week it was! Dances, moonlight strolls, and, finally, toward the end of camp, an invitation to accompany her to her dorm room. I said 'um . . . OK' and followed her onto the elevator with another dozen hormone-crazed teenagers and the oldest guard in the history of band-camp guards."

Plus a dash of description. Your tale should be vivid and include specific details. This could mean actual sights, sounds, and smells from your direct experience, or it could be the part of your story where your creative juices flow. Follow the adage of "show, don't tell" and give your listeners something concrete to imagine.

> "A hundred years old, at least, with eyebrows that jutted from his forehead like horns and cold blue eyes that peered into my very soul. I could almost hear him thinking, 'I know what you're up to, boy . . .'"

Sprinkle humor to taste. The greatest tales are best served with a helping of humor. Even a serious story benefits from a funny observation or silly added detail. If your audience is smiling, they're listening.

> "I imagined a torch-bearing horde of instructors descending upon Amanda's dorm room and dragging my bewildered, besotted self out into the cool West Chester night to face justice."

Finish strong. All stories should end with a definitive resolution, and the best tall tales have a lesson tucked in somewhere.

> "I looked from Amanda to the guard—then back to Amanda, then back to the guard, and as the elevator doors closed I whimpered 'I can't!' and jumped out. The last thing I saw was Amanda's shocked face disappearing behind the closing elevator doors. Our paths never crossed again, and to this day I've sworn if they ever discover time travel, I'm going to wait outside the elevator, and when 17-year-old me jumps out, I'm going to push him right back in."

Remember, any tale you tell should be appropriate for your grandchild's age. This tale of my failure to get lucky at band camp probably won't work for my granddaughter until she's thirty . . . or maybe ever!

Build Your Own Grandfather Story

You may remember tales spun by your grandfather, tales that alternated between extreme hardship and joyful innocence, tales of times when supporting a minimum wage made you a damn commie but everything cost less than a dollar so it didn't really matter. Now it's your turn! Use this handy story chart to fascinate your grandchild with incredible tales from the days of yore.

Beginning (pick 1)

Back in my day . . .

Did I ever tell you about the time . . .

That's nothing! One time . . .

I got *this* scar after . . .

Now, this was before . . .

Used to be, years ago, that . . .

Have I got a story for you! So . . .

Action (pick 1)

I used to walk past (up, by, down, to, etc.)

I could buy

I used to drive

I'd always watch

I jumped over (past, by, to, etc.)

Object (pick up to 3)

Trees as big as that

The elementary school

An unpaved road

Hoagie McGill's Garage

A drink at the soda fountain

A Buffalo nickel

My old collection of 45s

The drive-in theater

Intensifier (pick 1)

Six miles*, uphill both ways.

Through three feet of snow.

Whenever I damn well pleased.

Without anyone making a peep.

For a nickel.

Coup de grâce (pick 1)

You don't know how good you got it, kid!

Those were the good old days.

You'll never see that again.

They don't make 'em like that anymore.

Not bad for an old geezer, eh?

*All distances are variable. To calculate, multiply actual distance by age of youngest listener and round down.

Favorite Bedtime Stories for Grandfathers

Not sure which bedtime stories are best to get your grandkid off to sleepyland? The Poky Little Puppy and his ilk have hip new company nowadays. Turn the page for my grandchild-approved favorites.

Tips for Bedtime Reading

Plan on multiple stories. Rarely will one be enough. At the start of bedtime, tell your grandchild how many stories you will read before lights out.

Let him choose. Bedtime will go easier if you let him pick the book(s) he wants to hear.

Go with the flow. If one of the stories he's picked requires a lot of interactivity or action, start with that one. The final story should be quiet to help ease him into sleep.

Do it right. Show the pictures, use voices, and, most important, read slowly and quietly. Don't just mindlessly turn pages.

Make it a ritual. Story time is a special time, so try to do it each night that you spend with him.

Book	Author/Illustrator
Snoozers	Sandra Boyton
No Sleep for the Sheep!	Karen Beaumont Jackie Urbanovic
Goodnight Moon	Margaret Wise Brown Clement Hurd
Llama Llama Gram and Grandpa	Anne Dewdney
Pete the Cat: Rock On, Mom and Dad!	James Dean
Goodnight Engines	Denise Dowling Mortensen Melissa Iwai
Starry Safari	Linda Ashman Jeff Mack
Guess How Much I Love You	Sam McBratney Anita Jeram
I Love You, Grandpa	Jillian Harker Daniel Howarth

Description

Seven charming stories about bedtime with lots of colorful illustrations.

A sheep wants to get some sleep, but his friends won't let him. Lots of fun animal noises.

This classic has been handed down through generations. Your grandchild will likely read this to his grandchild someday!

One of the ever-growing Llama Llama series, this book features the titular hero's trip to visit his grandparents.

A special volume in the beloved kids' series that covers the importance of giving thanks.

A beautifully illustrated tale that walks through the nightly shutting down of many things that go.

An exciting action adventure filled with diverse animals that offers lots of opportunity to interact with your listener.

This treasured tale of love now comes in a pop-up format that's perfect to read aloud.

One of a series of Little Bear's adventures, this book includes Grandpa Bear helping out. It's a wonderful way to end the day with your grandbaby.

Proper Event Etiquette

One of the best ways to bet involved in your grand-child's life is to attend the events that are important to her. You probably went to dozens of games and performances when your kids were young, but it's likely been a decade or more. So here's a refresher on the dos and don'ts.

At the Game

Do bring extra water, a snack, and a few bandages just in case.

Don't enter the team area (dugout, bench, etc.) unless asked by a coach.

Do bring a positive attitude and cheer for your grand-child and her teammates.

Don't criticize your grandchild, her teammates, referees, coaches, and parents.

Do feel proud about your grandchild's involvement.

Don't brag about what a star your little athlete is, rattle off stats, or otherwise compare your grandchild to the other players (and don't take the bait if someone else does).

Do support and congratulate your grandchild after the game, win or lose.

Don't criticize or show anger if her team loses.

Do offer to help out or volunteer. These organizations usually need all the help they can get.

Don't take on more than you can handle. You might not have time to whip up homemade granola bars for every game, but perhaps you can man the snack bar for an hour.

> NOTE: Sports are a wonderful way for your grandchild to make friends and learn about teamwork and commitment while getting exercise and fresh air . . . but they're not for everyone. If your grandchild isn't interested in sports, don't force her into playing. Find something else she's interested in and move on!

On the Class Trip

Do bring an itinerary, written plan, or location map for the trip—and follow it.

Don't "wing it," even if you're familiar with the attraction. Stick to the plan and be back at the meet-up point on time.

Do get the phone numbers for the trip organizers, fellow chaperones, and, if possible, the parents of the children you're responsible for.

Don't stay quiet if there is a problem with a student. Let a teacher know as soon as possible.

Do pay attention. If you're at a busy location, it's easy to let your concentration slip. Take frequent head counts and mind your charges at all times.

Don't take on more than you can handle. If you don't have the stamina to chase after a gaggle of little ones on a blazing-hot day, beg off. There are other ways you can help!

Do let the kids have fun. This doesn't mean you can let them ride roughshod, but remember that this is a special occasion and, unless safety is at issue, let minor infractions slide.

Don't yell or publicly embarrass your charges. If a student crosses a line, pull him aside and speak to him individually.

Do keep the patter going. Let your inner teacher shine and share your knowledge about the topics at hand.

Don't contradict guides or teachers while they are sharing lessons, even if you think you're right.

At the Dance Recital/Play/Concert

Do bring your camera or cell phone and take lots of off-stage photos of your little one.

Don't take photos or videos during the event. Flash photography and camera lighting is distracting to performers and audience members alike.

Do cheer with vigor at the appropriate time (e.g., at the end of the piece rather than between movements).

Don't shout, hoot, or otherwise carry on midperformance when your grandchild enters the stage.

Do bring flowers or another gift and provide rave reviews to your little performer after the show.

Don't criticize or offer "improvement" suggestions to your grandchild, other performers, or directors.

The Grandfatherly Art of Gift Giving

There's nothing quite like seeing the joy on the face of a child when she unwraps something she desperately wants. The extra hugs and the occasional whispers of "you're the best" don't hurt either. But before you purchase something for your grandchild, consider these tips for gift-giving success.

Don't be a spoiler! If you have disposable income, the temptation to spoil your grandchild can be great. An occasional splurge is acceptable, but always getting her what she wants when she wants it could lead to unrealistic expectations and a sense of entitlement (or tantrums) later.

Be space conscious. When you buy your grandkid a gift, think of where she will store it. She might love a giant play-kitchen set with loads of the accessories, but if she lives in a small apartment with four other people, there might not be a spot for it, which can frustrate her parents. As much as possible, work with your child to figure out what gifts make sense.

Be consistent. If you have multiple grandchildren, don't play favorites. This doesn't mean you have to buy them the same exact things, but try your best to spend similarly on each child. There is no surer way to hurt feelings than to lavish expensive electronics upon one grandchild while giving another an envelope full of cereal-box tops!

Think long term. Toys break and lose parts. Movies and games fall out of style and get forgotten. But some gifts last forever. Instill a love of reading in your grandchild by giving the gift of books. Introduce her to a new hobby, something she can enjoy for a lifetime. And there's always cold, hard cash (or its equivalent; see the investment tips on page 90). Teach your grandchild about finances and budgets by setting up an account and buying individual shares of stocks or mutual funds. They may not seem like much at first, but she'll thank you later when she has money to fall back on.

Things to Do with Grandkids: Fun with Paper

It may sound like one of those classic grandfather chestnuts, but it's true: all you *really* need for fun is a single sheet of paper.

Airplanes

Use standard 8½-by-11-inch printer paper to design and build these, and then have contests for speed, distance, and flair. Try these two simple favorites.

For speed and distance, make the **Jetstream**.

1. Fold the sheet in half lengthwise to establish a center line and then unfold it.

2. Fold both top corners in toward the center line. You should have something that looks like a tall house.

3. Fold the new top corners (the bottom points of the house's roof) toward the center line to make roughly a steep-sided triangle.

4. Fold the sheet in half along the center line, and then create the wings by folding the two bottom

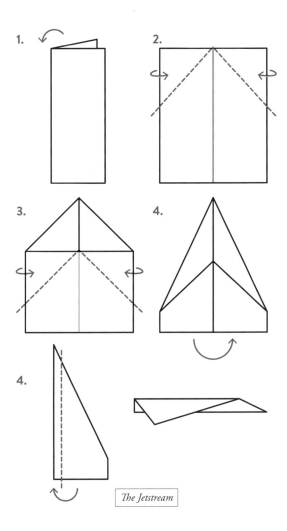

1.

2.

3.

4.

4.

The Jetstream

corners of the triangle back about 1 inch. Your finished product should rival the Concorde in sleek elegance and speed.

For a little pizzazz, make the **Tricky Flyer**.

1. Fold the top left down to meet the right edge of the sheet.

2. Fold the top right down to meet the left edge of the paper. You'll have something that looks like a small house.

3. Fold down the top point of the house's roof to meet the base of the roof.

4. Fold in half lengthwise, and then make the wings by folding each half out, leaving about ½ inch for the body of the airplane.

5. Create a ½-inch fold along the edge of each wing to make airfoils. Your finished product will have squared edges. It won't look like much, but when airborne it will loop and swirl like a drunken sparrow.

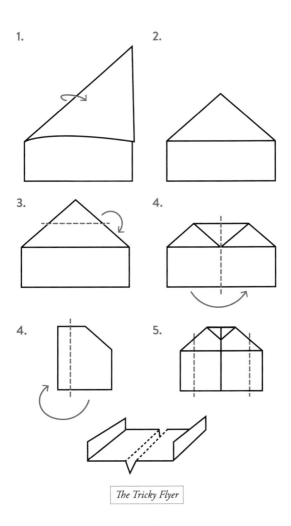

1.

2.

3.

4.

4.

5.

The Tricky Flyer

Swan

Origami, the ancient Japanese art of folding paper, doesn't have to be complicated. Build this swan in 7 easy steps.

1. Fold an 8-inch square of paper in half on the diagonal to create a center line and then unfold the paper.

2. Fold each top corner toward the center line, creating a kite shape. Fold the left and right corner toward the center line to form a diamond.

3. Fold the top point down to meet the two side points in the center of the diamond.

4. Fold about ¾ inch of the point up, making the head of the swan.

5. Fold the paper in half lengthwise; you should start seeing the swan take shape.

6. Gently position the neck forward and the head up. Your swan is ready for her close-up!

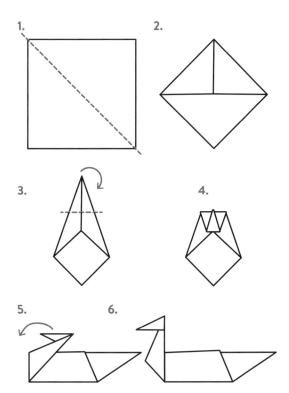

1.

2.

3.

4.

5.

6.

Swan

> **VARIATION:** After making the swan, have your grandchild help you create a family of cygnets using smaller squares of paper. Then playact a story together.

Hat

These are best made with larger sheets (like news-paper), but standard 8½-by-11-inch paper works too. Depending on the size and thickness of the paper, you may need a bit of tape.

1. Fold the paper in half widthwise.

2. Fold in half lengthwise to establish a center line and then unfold this fold. The area on either side of the center line will be roughly square.

3. Fold the top corners toward the center line to form a triangle with about an extra inch at the bottom. If you're using bigger paper, you may want to affix a little piece of tape where the two sides meet.

4. Fold the bottom inch of the paper up on each side, creating the base of the hat. Pull open and

wear (or if you prefer, float it in the bath as a boat.)

After you're done building, give the kids crayons, markers, and other crafting materials to decorate their creations.

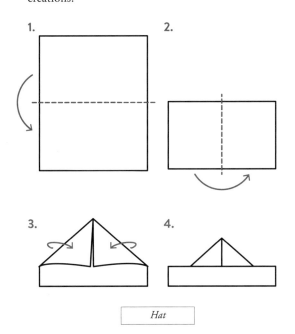

Hat

Things to Do with Grandkids: Rainy Day Edition

Maybe the power is out, or the internet is wonky, or you're living in a dystopian hellscape with nothing to do. Whether the reason is rain or something else, the grandkids are bored and you are looking for a way to pass the time. Pry the smartphone/television remote/gaming controller from their fingers and try one of these five low-impact classics (all good for groups of kids under age 12).

I Spy. You don't even have to leave your seat for this one. Identify an object of a certain color, and announce "I spy with my little eye, something . . . blue," and let children take turns guessing the object. Guessing continues until someone gets it right, and then the guesser becomes the "spyer." I Spy is a great way to teach observational skills and colors to kids younger than age 6. It's also fun to play on long road trips.

PopPop May I? Similar to Simon Says, this game requires a bit of space. Participants line up in a row, and a caller stands across from them at the "finish line" and calls out instructions to individual players to take a certain number of steps. (For example, "Johnny, take three steps.") The catch is, before the player moves, he must ask the caller "PopPop, may I?" If the caller says yes, the player can proceed. (So if Johnny responds, "PopPop, may I take three steps?" he's free and clear to walk forward!) But if he moves without asking, he has to go back to the start. Whoever crosses the finish line first wins. This game is an excellent way to teach manners, and if you give the kids a vacuum cleaner or dust brush, you could even get a clean floor out of it.

Huckle Buckle Beanstalk. The kids cover their eyes while you hide a small object (nothing valuable!), and then the search begins. Guide them with hints ("You're getting warmer"). The child who finds the object calls out "Huckle Buckle Beanstalk" to alert all others that the search is over. The finder becomes the hider, and now you take a turn searching with the others.

NOTE: If your grandkids are approaching double digits (so about age 8 and up), you can try a treasure hunt variant of this game. Hide the object and write a series of clues and riddles containing hints (or even parts of a map). It takes a little effort, but you can keep their interest for a whole afternoon *and* keep their brains working.

Dress-Up. Break out old Halloween costumes, clothes you've been meaning to donate, or Grandmom's old costume jewelry—it's time for a dress-off! Mix and match, don't be afraid to be silly, and have the camera ready for blackmail material later.

Essential Skills for the Great Outdoors

As a grandfather you have an endless supply of fun activities and experiences to share with your grandkid, but little compares to teaching him about the wonders of the great outdoors. Even if you can't tell a bumblebee from a hummingbird, consider an outdoor outing with your little one and remember these tips.

Get ready—mentally and physically. Dress appropriately for the activity. For a hike in the woods, think about long pants, a lightweight long-sleeve shirt, and a hat. Supportive, well-fitting shoes are a must. Remember, cell phones are ubiquitous now but the signals aren't, so bring a map (and know how to read it!) and make sure folks know where you're going and for about how long you'll be gone. And know your limits. If you're completely sedentary, take some preparatory walks before you embark on this great adventure to build stamina and break in any new gear.

Pick a location. Many states have excellent websites that detail state parks and other locations with hiking trails, including difficulty level and suggestions of flora and fauna to look for. The National Park Service website (www.nps.gov) offers a complete listing of trails across the country, including detailed maps. Find something that's appropriately difficult for you and your grandchild and that includes scenery or history of interest to you both.

Pack light (but not too light). Water is a must, as are bug repellent and sunblock. You might also bring a small first aid kit, binoculars, a bag for trash, a knife or multipurpose tool, and a compass (probably not necessary, but a great learning tool for your grandkid). Snacks, too, are a welcome addition—they call it trail mix for a reason! Put it all in a backpack, and make sure you can handle the weight. If your grandchild is old enough, let him share the burden in his own pack.

Take your time. There's no need to rush. Make frequent stops to take in the view and point out sights and sounds to your grandchild: interesting flowers or plants, birdcalls, animal tracks, the strata of the forest, the impact of erosion in the desert, the call of the brook. Bring along nature books that can help you identify what you're seeing, or take photos that you can review later together to discover what you found.

Check for ticks. After your hike, check yourself and your grandchild for ticks around the feet and ankles (including the top few inches below the socks), along the hairline, and around the neck and shoulders.

At home, do a more thorough check, including under the private areas, in the armpits, and behind the ears. Recruit your grandkid's parent or grandmother to help if appropriate.

How to Remove a Tick

The Centers for Disease Control and Prevention recommends the following steps for removing a tick.

1. Using fine-tipped tweezers, grasp the tick as close to the skin surface as possible.

2. Pull slowly and firmly towards its hindquarters. Don't twist or jerk as you pull.

3. Clean the bite area with rubbing alcohol, and wash your hands with soap and water.

4. Dispose of the tick by putting it in alcohol, placing it in a sealed bag, or flushing it down the toilet.

5. Look out for signs of infection, including a rash or fever. If these occur, see your doctor.

How to Use Social Media (and Technology in General)

Modern technology allows us to stay connected to friends and family across the world and to share life's joys and tribulations with an ever-expanding network of friends. Unfortunately, the gadgets and platforms that allow us to chat face-to-face with a loved one who's miles away also make it possible for sensitive personal information to be accessed by a rogues' gallery of bad actors.

Social media has become an integral part of life. Many of our children and grandchildren have never lived in a world where it didn't exist; but to grandfathers of a certain age, it can be fraught with mystery and danger. Here's how to use it right.

Should you friend your grandchildren? Absolutely! One of the best parts of social media is the ability to connect to family, so take advantage. Younger grandkids will likely readily accept your request. As they reach adolescence, there might be some hesitancy, but it doesn't hurt to ask.

You might be thinking, "why not friend my grand-kid's friends too?" After all, what better way to find out what's going on in your grandchild's life than to see what her friends are up to? Your reasoning is sound, but let the friends take the lead on this. If they reach out to you, it's fine. If you reach out to them, you could come across as a creepy old man stalking young people online.

Watch your commenting. Teens put a lot of their lives (some would say too much) online, not all of which you will approve of. Refrain from scolding them online; posting unwanted commentary is a short road to the unfriended zone. And who knows, there could be subtext or stories behind their content that you don't understand. If something seriously upsets or worries you, share your concerns with the parents.

Resist the overshare. Think twice before posting that adorable bath-time photo of your grandchild or sharing that side-splitting story about the time she lost her shoes in a mud puddle. What you might be considering a lovely moment could embarrass your grandchild (which is her parents' job!). If you have any doubt about whether something will cause your grandchild discomfort, ask for permission. And if she asks you to take down something you've already posted, honor that request.

On a similar note, watch what you post about

yourself. The internet is omnipresent, and if you're sharing something not for public consumption you can't assume it will remain within your circle of friends. Embarrassing information can spread awfully fast.

Finally, be cautious about posting things that let people know your house is empty (such as when you're on vacation) or that you're home alone (especially as you get older).

Just be yourself. You may think your grandkids would appreciate you trying to adopt their slang. Don't fall for that trap. Simply be the adorable middle-aged or older gentleman you are. Trust me, by the time you figure out how to use the vernacular correctly, it will change again!

Believe nothing. The founder of FaceSpace won't donate $10 for every time you share his post. That meme with a damning quote by your most hated politician probably came from some 'bot. And that flying monkey video is a complete fabrication. A lot of bad information is floating around the internet. Save yourself and your grandchild a ton of embarrassment and find a reputable site or news source (I'm a big believer in Snopes.com) to fact-check something before you share it.

Other Technology Safety Tips

Don't click it! Never click a link in an email, even if the source seems legitimate. Bad guys use legit-seeming email links and attachments to collect your personal log-ins or install programs on your computer that can gather sensitive information. Instead, only log into your accounts by entering the web address directly into your browser (or using bookmarks or shortcuts).

Watch out for new friends. If you get a connection request from someone you don't know, don't accept it without doing some digging first. If you can't find someone you know to vouch for the person, delete the request. It's not uncommon for hackers to use phony accounts to ensnare unsuspecting folks.

Pop-ups are no good for Pop-Pops! One common scam involves ads that pop up and invite you to click a button. The more nefarious of these will make you believe that your computer is infected with a virus and give you a phone number to call to fix it; and the "tech support" on the other end of the line will not only charge you to "fix" the problem but will download more spyware as well. If you get one of these messages, close the entire window. And hire real tech support to scan your system for viruses.

How to Plan a Family Vacation

Unless you happen to own a private, personal getaway spot, vacations are expensive. Even a simple beach vacation or a week in the woods costs thousands of dollars, which can be steep for a young family just starting out or an older couple on a fixed income. Combining resources can be a way to offset these costs. Plus, a joint vacation is a wonderful way to connect with your kids and grandkids.

A multiple-family escape requires extra planning, however. Here are suggestions to help you pull it off.

Work together. As much as possible, make sure all adults are involved in planning. Agree on a rough budget and draft a list of destinations that all parties agree on. Remember, different generations like different things, so try to settle on a location that has something for everyone.

Make sure you "right size" things. That snug little cabin may have worked for you and your wife, or when your kids were little and you didn't mind close quarters. But with multiple adults in the mix, you have to consider things ranging from different sleep patterns to privacy. Make sure everyone has enough room to spread out and relax.

Split the burdens. Decide what food and gear you need for the trip, and agree ahead of time on who is bringing what so that you don't end up with four heads of lettuce and no salad bowl. Divvy up chores so that everyone contributes fairly to the cooking and cleaning (as is age-appropriate, of course), and plan in advance when to dine in and when to splurge on meals out. Email and file sharing make it easy to assemble a checklist that everyone can see.

Plan ahead. Cook a few easy-to-freeze meals like baked ziti or mac and cheese ahead of time, so that all you need to do at mealtime is throw it in the oven. Decide sleeping arrangements before you arrive at your destination—whoever is paying the most gets first dibs. (Ties are decided by age.)

Vive la différence . . . If you're a "get up with the sun and tackle the world" type but your kids and grandkids are more the "sit around and let the world wash over you" sort, you're bound to experience tension. Don't assume that when you're on vacation you'll all be on the same schedule or even want to do the same activities. Togetherness is nice, but allow everyone to relax and have fun in the way that suits them. And remember: it's your vacation too. Make sure you have fun.

. . . but set expectations. That said, try to schedule at least one event—a meal, excursion, or activity—for the whole family. Doing so will let you celebrate your time together and help create shared memories. Communicate times and locations clearly so everyone is on the same page.

Have a contingency plan. Even the best-laid plans can run afoul of inopportune circumstances, unplanned guests, and less-than-perfect weather, so be ready to be flexible. Bring playing cards and board games, extra sheets and pillows, and ingredients for a couple easy-to-prepare backup meals just in case.

Pack your grandfather hat. Find an activity that you can do with your grandkids that they'll remember as a special moment with Pop-Pop, like an early morning fishing trip on the lake or building a sand castle. For extra brownie points, give your child the gift of grown-up time by offering to babysit the kids for a few hours one night.

Six Classic Grandfatherly Tricks and Pranks

One of the inarguable rights of grandfathers everywhere is to play silly mind games with the newest generation. Chances are you've had at least one of these things done to you when you were young, so now it's time to pass 'em down.

Got your nose! Very gently grasp your grandkid's nose between your index and middle fingers. Pull your hand away, and slide your thumb between those two fingers, leaving only the tip exposed. Show her the pad side of your grasped thumb and call out "I got your nose!" Be sure to put it back on her face when you're done.

Thumb removal. With one hand, hold the four fingers tightly together and bend the thumb in toward your palm so that the bottom knuckle is slightly exposed (viewed palm-side down, your thumb should be almost invisible). Sharply bend the thumb on your other hand toward your palm and place your index finger over the knuckle (imagine a slightly smooshed "OK" symbol). Align both of your thumbs at the center knuckle, using your index finger to obscure where the two knuckles meet, then slide your second hand over the top of the first (away from the wrist, toward the fingers). Practice this in a mirror a few times before performing it for your grandchild; it will look like you are smoothly and painlessly removing your thumb.

What's that in your ear? For this classic sleight of hand, palm a small coin, then reach behind your grandchild's head and transfer the coin so it's grasped between your thumb and forefinger. Then pull your hand back from behind her head (try to brush her ear with the coin as you do to really sell the trick). Hold the coin up in amazement and proclaim, "I found this in your ear." Those with better legerdemain skills can pull coins from other places (like the nose). In all cases, your grandkid gets to keep the coin, provided she's old enough not to put it in her mouth.

Cracking an egg. Approach your grandchild from behind and place a loosely clenched fist on the crown of her head. Use your other hand to *gently* slap your fist to mimic the cracking of the egg, and then slowly trail your fingers down both sides of her head to simulate the yolk trickling down.

The thousand-pound ring finger. Have your grandchild place her hand on the table, bending her middle finger under the palm and leaving the thumb and other fingers extended. One at a time, state a realistic weight for each finger, leaving the ring finger for last. After the others, state "your ring finger weighs a thousand pounds—try to lift it." For most people, the tendons between fingers are attached and they'll be unable to raise it.

Pull my finger? If you're a man of a certain age, chances are you have gas. And it's a known fact that 99.999 percent of kids love farts. What better way to combine the two in this grossest of rituals? Chances are this particular prank will not be sanctioned by your spouse or your grandchild's parents. Use it sparingly, and do not perform it in public.

Five Favorite Fictional Grandfathers

Now that you're a grandfather, you may feel relegated to the role of background character in the family narrative. But plenty of novels, movies, and other stories portray the grandfather as the one who shook stuff up, made things happen, or saved the day. Here are some top fictional pop-pops to look to for inspiration.

The Grandfather from *The Princess Bride*

Portrayed by Peter Falk in the classic Rob Reiner film adaptation of the novel by William Goldman, this is the perfect grandfather. Returning each day to read his sick grandson a tale of fencing, fighting, and true love (even the icky kissing parts), he does such a fabulous job that he's asked back to read the story again.

Grandpa Joe from *Charlie and the Chocolate Factory*

You won't find a more supportive grandfather than the hobbled old Grandpa Joe from Roald Dahl's classic book. A case study in both faith (after all, he's the one who convinced Charlie to keep looking for the final golden ticket) and staying young at heart, Grandpa Joe was the perfect escort for the young Master Bucket's visit through Willie Wonka's wacky world.

Edwin Hoover from *Little Miss Sunshine*

You wouldn't think a foul-mouthed drug addict who dies before the third act belongs on this list, but Grandpa Hoover teaches the young Olive a good lesson about loving who you are and being yourself.

Richard DeTamble from *The Time Traveler's Wife*

Although a minor character in Audrey Niffenegger's beautiful novel about destiny and hope, Alba's violin-playing grandfather has a redemptive arc that takes him from a distant alcoholic to his time-traveling granddaughter's key mentor.

Royal Tenenbaum from *The Royal Tenenbaums*

No, the self-absorbed paterfamilias of the Tennenbaum clan trying to con his way back to his estranged family's good graces by faking illness doesn't exactly scream "Good Grandpa." But Royal learns an important lesson along the way and leaves his family in a better place by the end of Wes Anderson's quirky film.

Six Great Ways to Bond with Your Grandkid

If the occasional visit or babysitting gig isn't enough for you, you may want to find other ways to stay involved in your grandchild's life (and maybe help out his parents in the process). Here are some ideas.

Volunteer. Becoming a coach, scout leader, or school chaperone allows you to spend time with your grandchild while helping your community. Volunteering also can connect you with like-minded people and you might learn something new.

Schedule field trips. Museums, zoos, even just a day in the park are great ways to share time with your grandchild, with the added bonuses that he might learn something and you'll get a bit of exercise. Research the attraction ahead of time, and share interesting tidbits with him ("Did you know lemurs come from Madagascar and their society is run by females?").

Everybody eats. Kids love food. You love food. What better way to bond than over food? Make it a regular occurrence: a pizza night, a Sunday brunch, etc. Chat about his soccer team or Model UN summit, and share your news of the week.

Share your hobbies. Maybe you like building models, or completing puzzles, or writing poetry. Why not introduce your grandchild to that side of you and get him involved? If you have a regular project, let him pitch in. Or set up a parallel project so he can work alongside you. As always, make sure the activity is age appropriate.

Share his hobbies. Find out what your grandchild is interested in and learn about it. Check out his favorite book series or television series, and have regular discussions about plot points. Ask him to demystify this whole YouTube thing and how to use it. Have him play you his favorite song (and try to keep a straight face).

Just find your "thing." Maybe none of the suggestions above work for you and your grandkid. Make it your goal to find one thing that you can share with him on a regular basis. It could be a movie night, or a trip to the hardware store, or helping a political campaign, or whatever else you enjoy together. By establishing a shared interest, you're helping create memories that will last a lifetime.

How to Be the Guy They Confide In

Everyone needs someone they can turn to for advice, or maybe just a sympathetic ear. Your grandchildren are no different, and if you want to have the honor of playing this important role in your grandchild's life, keep the following tips in mind.

Walk the walk. If you want your grandkid to come to you for advice, it helps to have your stuff together. That doesn't mean you have to have all the answers (really, who does?), but you should be comfortable enough with yourself to inspire confidence in your grandchild.

Be approachable. Make sure your grandkid know that your door is always open. Share your stories—both successes and failures—with him and he'll come to see you as someone he can trust who's also human. Your relationship with your children helps here; if your grandchild sees his parents coming to you for guidance, he'll feel comfortable doing the same.

Be supportive. Above all things, make sure your grandchild knows that you're here for him. If he's worried about something, don't belittle or demean his concerns, even if they seem trivial. And though humor is usually a good tool to bring a smile or diffuse a tense conversation, be careful. Cracking a joke at the wrong time could make your grandchild believe you're trivializing his feelings.

No judgment. If your grandchild comes to you discuss a mistake he made, provide constructive feedback and do not criticize. Talk through the points that led to the error, and steer him toward the path of correction. Provide honest feedback leavened with kindness, and don't get angry. Remember, you were young and stupid once too.

Timing is everything. If the discussion is fraught with emotion, the lessons can wait. Make sure your grandchild is safe, comfort him as necessary, and consider reserving the constructive feedback until a time when emotions aren't as high.

Be an active listener. Sometimes the most important thing you can do is simply listen. As an adult who has seen a lot of life, you may be tempted to fast-forward straight to the solution. But it is vital that you pay attention to a child's words and be an engaged listener. Ask questions, look for nonverbal cues, and make sure your grandchild understands that you're taking him and his concerns seriously.

How to Leave Your Legacy

Not to be completely morbid, but you are going to die. We all are. And it's very possible your grandkids will live a big chunk of their lives without you. This may seem sad, but you have an opportunity to create a meaningful legacy. Here are ways to stay alive in their hearts.

Keep a journal. It doesn't have to be anything fancy—a regular collection of notes and observations, whether in a physical journal or an online equivalent, will do. Include your perspective on significant events or personal notes to your loved ones. Your family can revisit and share your memories and stories forever. (You can find "line a day" journals at most office supply stores.)

Document visual history. Photographs are wonderful for chronicling life's passing. Print your favorites; digital photos are great, but in twenty years, when the technology's completely changed, those files might be unusable. A quick trip to the drugstore photo center can ensure that the memories and stories behind those photos will be around for years. Organize them in an album and label them with important details, like who's in the photo and where it was taken.

Record and report. You've probably already shared a lifetime of stories with your grandchild. Some may be remembered and shared for generations, and others may be forgotten. Consider telling them again, and ask your family to record you on audio or video. Hearing the stories in your voice—and seeing your face—is something they will treasure.

Tend to the tree. Modern genealogy sites like Ancestry .com have made family histories a business. You don't have to be a dedicated family historian, but even a little bit of research can turn up treasures that you can share with your grandchild. As an added bonus, these sites allow users to upload photos and important documents that you can share with generations to come.

Hopefully when you do shuffle off this mortal coil, you're able to do so after a lifetime filled with love and laughter. Those memories that you've shared, the stories that can be passed down through the generations, the good life you have lived are the greatest gift you can give your family.

Acknowledgments

Thanks to Quirk Books, especially Blair Thornburgh, for giving me this opportunity.

Thank you to Shawn, Dave, and Carol for Grumpa, Gramps, and Grand Dude, respectively.

Thank you to Sarah, Rebecca, and Hannah for your patience while I figured out the whole "dad" thing. I couldn't ask for better daughters.

Thank you, Maureen, for being my partner in grandparently crime. Lily is a lucky little lady with you as a MomMom.

Thank you to my Mom for being a great mother, a great grandmother, *and* a great great-grandmother.

And most of all, thank you Daddy and Jimbo for giving me something to aspire to. Any grandfatherly wisdom found in the preceding pages, I learned from you first. I miss you both.